6. Pray for God's help. You *need* God's help in order to understand what you study in the Bible. Psalm 119:18 would be an appropriate verse for you to take to God in prayer.

7. *Class teachers using this course for group study will find some helpful suggestions on page 47.*

how to take the self-check tests

Each lesson is concluded with a test designed to help you evaluate what you have learned.

1. Review the lesson carefully in the light of the self-check test questions.

2. If there are any questions in the self-check test you cannot answer, perhaps you have written into your lesson the wrong answer from your Bible. Go over your work carefully to make sure you have filled in the blanks correctly.

3. When you think you are ready to take the self-check test, do so without looking up the answers.

4. Check your answers to the self-check test carefully with the answer key given on page 48.

5. If you have any questions wrong, your answer key will tell you where to find the correct answer in your lesson. Go back and locate the right answers. Learn by your mistakes!

apply what you have learned to your own life

In this connection, read carefully JAMES 1:22-25. It is only as you apply your lessons to your own life that you will really grow in grace and increase in the knowledge of God.

INTRODUCTION

The author

That the author of this Gospel was Luke is indicated by the fact that he wrote Acts (as seen by the "we" sections), and both the Gospel of Luke and Acts were addressed to the same person (LUKE 1:3; ACTS 1:1). Scholars from Irenaeus (second century) to the present day agree as well.

The date and place of writing

Some who would attempt to discredit the prophecy of the destruction of Jerusalem (LUKE 21:20-40) place the date of the writing after A.D. 70, the date Jerusalem was destroyed. However, Acts must have been written before A.D. 70 since it was produced during the lifetime of Paul (probably A.D. 63). The Gospel was written before Acts (ACTS 1:1), probably in A.D. 60. The place where it was written may have been Caesarea or Rome. Perhaps Luke began it in one place and finished it in another.

The distinctions of Luke

Some who have asked, "Why four Gospels?" have discovered that Luke's Gospel gives us a more complete picture of our Saviour and His purposes. There is unity of subject, yet diversity of treatment. This helps us see more clearly all that God has intended for us (see chart).

The theme of Luke is Jesus Christ the Son of Man. This is not to obscure His deity nor obtrude His humanity, but rather to lift up the manhood of Christ. Thus, the forerunner John the Baptist is described, the birth of Christ with shepherds is detailed, and the obedience and prayer life of Christ is discussed.

This Gospel is not only distinct in theme, but also in material. Most of nine chapters (9:51–18:35) are not found in any other Gospel. Also distinctive are the following: six out of the twenty miracles; nineteen out of the twenty-three parables, including the prodigal son and the good Samaritan; the infancy details of John the Baptist and Christ; the emphasis on prayer; medical matters and terminology; and the walk of Christ to Emmaus. Certainly much revelation would be lost without this Gospel, and much spiritual truth is lost without an adequate study of it.

The outline of Luke

1. The Advent of Christ 1:1–4:30
   (Lessons 1 and 2)
2. The Ministry of Christ 4:31–9:50
   (Lessons 3 and 4)
3. The Rejection of Christ 9:51–11:54
   (Lesson 5)
4. The Instruction of Christ 12:1–19:48
   (Lessons 6 to 9)
5. The Suffering of Christ 20:1–23:56
   (Lessons 10 and 11)
6. The Resurrection of Christ 24:1-53
   (Lesson 12)

THE DISTINCTIONS OF THE GOSPELS

	Themes	*Key Verses*	*Symbols* (Ezekiel 1:10)	*Prophecies*	*Genealogies*	*Addressees*	*Endings*
MATTHEW	Christ as King	Matthew 21:5	The Lion (Supreme Strength)	The Righteous Branch (Jeremiah 23:5; 33:15)	Son of David Son of Abraham (Matthew 1:1)	Jews	Resurrection (Proof of Messiahship)
MARK	Christ as Servant	Mark 10:45	The Ox (Lowly Servant)	The Servant The Branch (Zechariah 3:8)	None	Romans	Ascension (Exaltation of Servant)
LUKE	Christ as the Son of Man	Luke 19:10	The Man	The man whose name is the Branch (Zechariah 6:12)	Adam (Luke 3:38)	Greeks	Spirit Promised (Man's Enablement)
JOHN	Christ as the Son of God	John 20:31	The Eagle (Heavenliness, Deity)		Eternal (John 1:1)	Church	Second Coming Promised (Church's Hope)

Luke 3rd Book of NT

Luke was a Physician — Co worker Paul
was a Gentile and a proselyte | Written before
a man of education + Culture A D 58-60

Lesson 1

Manuscripts
Uncial | Scripture pg 1145
Unger Dict.
274 are known
Most important is called
Codex Vaticanus
Lib. in Rome Since 1481 AD 340
759 leaves

The Birth of Christ

1:1—2:52

The preface of Luke 1:1-4

1. Describe the purpose Luke had in writing this Gospel.

1:4 to Theophilus — To bring us to God
To give honor to them to Whom honor is due.
He was moved by the Holy Spirit

The announcement of John's birth 1:5-25

John the Baptist was the forerunner of Christ, and the man and his message were predicted in the Old Testament (Isaiah 40:3-5; Malachi 3:1).

2. Why were Zacharias and his wife called "righteous before God" (1:6)?

Romans 10:5 because Zacharias and Elisabeth
live by the law of moses, they were a religious couple

3. Although a person may be blameless before the law, what is he before God?

Ecclesiastes 7:20 Holy

4. What did the Old Testament believer do, having sinned, that would make him blameless or righteous before God?

Leviticus 4:27-35 bring offering with out blemish
for his sins

5. To whom did these offerings look forward?

John 1:29 The Lamb of God (Jesus)

6. What three men were named before they were born?

Name by angels

GENESIS 17:19 Isaac

LUKE 1:13 John

LUKE 2:21 JESUS

7. In whose sight was John the Baptist to be great?

1:15 God

8. Who else spoke of his greatness?

7:28 JESUS

9. Who else is commanded to be filled with the Holy Spirit and not with strong drink?

EPHESIANS 5:18 Believers (The Gentiles)

10. Describe the work of John. Repent from Sin

1:16; compare 1:76 Prepare Jesus way

11. What was the name of the angel who appeared to Zacharias?

1:19 Gabriel

12. Who in Old Testament times had a conversation with this angel?

DANIEL 9:21-23 Daniel

13. Give the reason Zacharias was not able to speak.

1:20 He did not believe God's word

The announcement of Jesus' birth 1:26-38

14. What was to be the sign of the Saviour's coming into the world?

ISAIAH 7:14 A Virgin Shall have A Son

15. When was Mary found with child of the Holy Ghost?

MATTHEW 1:18 before Joseph & Mary Came together

16. Why was His name Jesus (1:31)?

MATTHEW 1:21 To Save his Peo from sin

17. Whose throne is Christ to receive?

1:32; compare PSALM 132:11 Lord

18. When will the throne of David again be established on the earth?

REVELATION 1:7, 8 When Jesus come

19. How long will the kingdom of Christ last?

1:33; compare REVELATION 11:15 forever

20. In what state or condition are we all born?

PSALM 51:5 In my Mother Womb

21. Why could not the Saviour be conceived through a man?

JOB 14:4 Because man is Consider unclean

22. What title, therefore, could be given to Jesus? Son of God

1:35 King of King Lord of Lord

The visit of Mary 1:39-56

23. Because Mary was to be the mother of our Lord, what was she called? HAND maiden

1:42; compare 1:48 Mother of Jesus

Mary is not called the blesser, but rather is the one blessed. She is not an object of worship (compare 11:27, 28; MATTHEW 12:46-50).

24. What did Mary as well as other women need?

1:47 Holy Spirit

25. Who was this Saviour?

2:11 JESUS CHRIST

The advent of John 1:57-80

26. When was Zacharias' mouth opened?

1:64; compare 1:20 Immediately

27. What did Zacharias understand to be the immediate purpose of the Saviour's coming into the world ?

1:68; compare Romans 3:24 To Redeem his People

28. Who is it that sits in darkness (1:79)?

John 3:19 SATAN (EVIL)

29. What is the only light that can penetrate this darkness?

John 1:9 Jesus

The advent of Jesus 2:1-52

30. What was prophesied concerning Bethlehem (2:4)? A ruler

Micah 5:2; John 7:42 Christ come (Son of man) from seed of David

31. What did the swaddling clothes suggest (2:7)?

Isaiah 53:2; II Corinthians 8:9 To Keep him warm

32. What was significant about Jesus being found by humble shepherds (2:8)?

John 10:11 He is a Shepherd

33. What was the glory that shone round about the angels (2:9)?

Exodus 16:10; 40:34, 35 Pillar of fire (a wall of fire)

34. What is said about those who continue to spread good tidings (2:10)?

Romans 10:15 They are Sent

35. For what was Bethlehem noted in olden times (2:11)?

II Samuel 23:15 City of David

36. Of what is this significant? If any one thrist he would give Them living water

JOHN 4:10 living water

37. How many would have the peace Jesus brought to earth (2:14)?

ROMANS 5:1 All who have faith

38. Give the reason Jesus was circumcised according to the law (2:21; compare LEVITICUS 12:3).

GALATIANS 4:4, 5 ______

39. Why was the offering of two turtledoves accepted by God in place of a lamb (2:24)?

LEVITICUS 12:8 Because it was the Law of the Lord

40. What was the consolation for which Simeon was waiting (2:25)?

2:38 ______

41. Before whose face had God prepared this salvation?

2:31; compare PSALM 98:2 ______

42. Why did not Simeon pronounce blessing upon the child as well as the parents (2:34)?

HEBREWS 7:7 ______

43. How soon did the wisdom of Christ begin to attract attention?

2:42, 43, 47 ______

44. What did prophecy have to say about His wisdom (2:40)?

ISAIAH 11:2, 3 ______

45. What did Paul later say about His wisdom?

COLOSSIANS 2:3 ______

46. Why was Jesus about His Father's business so early in life (2:49)?

JOHN 9:4 ______

47. What business did Jesus follow at Nazareth (2:51)?

MARK 6:3 ____________________

48. What admonition is given to all Christian children?

EPHESIANS 6:1, 2 Honor your mother + Father you will have long life

49. What is the best way to win the favor of God and man (2:52)?

ROMANS 14:18 righteous, peace in joy in the H.S.

50. What plan did Solomon prescribe?

PROVERBS 3:3, 4 have Love in your heart

51. If we cannot have the favor of men, of what should we make sure?

ACTS 7:9, 10 we have God in our heart

check-up time No. 1

You have just studied some important truths about the birth of Christ. Review your study by rereading the questions and your written answers. If you wish, you may use the self-check test as an aid in reviewing your lesson. If you aren't sure of an answer, reread the Scripture portion given to see if you can find the answer. Then take this test to see how well you understand important truths you have studied.

In the right-hand margin write "True" or "False" after each of the following statements.

1. Moses was named before he was born. F
2. The angel Gabriel announced the birth of John to his mother Elisabeth. F
3. All believers are to be filled with the Holy Spirit. T
4. Jesus is to receive the throne of David. T
5. The kingdom of Christ will last forever. T
6. Mary, the mother of Jesus, needed a Saviour. T
7. The home into which Jesus was born was wealthy. F
8. Simeon knew that Christ would come into the world. T
9. Jesus started the work of His Father late in life. F
10. Jesus increased in wisdom, stature, and deity. F

Turn to page 96 and check your answers.

LESSON 2

The Presentation of Christ

3:1—4:30

The ministry of John 3:1-20

1. How many high priests were there at that time?

3:2 1 Jesus Christ

This shows the religious degeneracy of the time, for this office was bought and sold. The message of both John and Jesus was greatly needed.

2. What must one do to repent (3:3)?

ISAIAH 55:7 Turn from their wicked ways

3. Describe what it means to prepare the way (3:4).

ISAIAH 57:14; 62:10 ______

4. To what does the bringing down of mountains and filling of valleys probably refer (3:5)?

1:51-53 ______

5. What did Christ come to do in His first advent?

3:6; compare 2:30; MATTHEW 1:21; JOHN 1:29 ______

6. How far did the news of Christ's saving work travel in the first century?

ROMANS 10:18 East to West

7. Who else spoke of a generation of vipers (3:7)?

MATTHEW 12:34 ~~[illegible]~~ John

8. What does this mean?

JOHN 8:44 ______

9. By whose power alone can we bring forth fruit unto God (3:8)?

GALATIANS 5:22-24 ______

10. Why was it useless for the Jews to boast of their ancestry (3:8)?

13:28 ______

11. Since the work of the cross, what is the answer to "What must we do" (3:10)?

ACTS 16:30, 31 ______

12. Whose baptism was Christ to give?

3:16 ______

13. For what did the promise of this baptism wait?

ACTS 2:33 ______

14. What did this baptism accomplish?

I CORINTHIANS 12:13 ______

15. To what does the fire refer (3:16)? ~~Tongues of fire~~

ACTS 2:3 Holy Spirit Tongues of fire

16. Of whom is fire a symbol?

ISAIAH 4:4 Spirit

17. If one will not have the fire of the Holy Ghost, what other fire will he be sure to receive?

MATTHEW 25:41, 46 fire prepared by the Devil

18. Where did Herod put John?

3:20 ______

The baptism of Jesus 3:21, 22

19. Why was Jesus baptized (3:21)?

HEBREWS 2:17 To be a High Priest

20. On this important occasion, what was Jesus doing?

3:21 ______

21. What did the baptism of Christ signify to John? son of God

JOHN 1:33 testimony that Jesus is the ~~Christ~~

22. Who was evidently an unseen witness of Jesus' baptism?

4:3 ______

The genealogy of Jesus 3:23-38

23. Whose son did the people at Nazareth believe Jesus to be?

4:16, 22; compare MATTHEW 13:54, 55 ______

24. By whom had He been conceived?

1:35 Holy spirit

It should be observed that Matthew's account (MATTHEW 1:1-17), which unquestionably gives the lineage of Joseph, states that Joseph was begat by Jacob. Luke's genealogy, which is different throughout, does not say, "Heli begat Joseph" but "Joseph the son of Heli," the word *son* being supplied by the translators. Jewish authorities tell us Luke's genealogy is that of Mary, whose father was Heli, who was a descendant of David through Nathan. As Joseph's father, Jacob was a descendant of David through Solomon. Thus, Joseph was Heli's son-in-law, but this term had not been invented and the term *son* was used uniformly to cover this relationship.

25. Who is the first man to whom Luke relates Christ?

3:38 ______

The testing of Jesus 4:1-13

26. Who led Jesus into the wilderness?

4:1 ______________________________

27. What companions did Jesus have in the wilderness?

MARK 1:13 ______________________________

28. Who else was alone with God forty days (4:2)?

EXODUS 24:18 ______________________________

29. Who else had a personal encounter with the devil?

GENESIS 3:1, 15 ______________________________

30. Why did Christ have to be tempted?

HEBREWS 2:17, 18 ______________________________

31. What did Satan want Christ to do first, to show He was the Son of God?

4:3 ______________________________

32. When was the suggestion of doubt as to His being the Son of God thrown at Him again?

MATTHEW 27:40 ______________________________

33. What weapon did Jesus use on the devil?

4:4; compare EPHESIANS 6:17 ______________________________

34. What is the best way for us to meet the devil?

PSALM 119:11 ______________________________

35. On what occasion had God proved this same promise to the Israelites?

DEUTERONOMY 8:3 ______________________________

36. What was Satan going to give Christ if He would but worship him?

4:5 ______________________________

37. What did Jesus call the devil?

John 12:31 ____________________

38. Describe the future of the devil.

Revelation 20:10 ____________________

39. What better way did Jesus have for coming into possession of the world (4:8)?

Psalm 2:8 ____________________

40. What was the third request of the devil?

4:9 ____________________

41. What words did Satan omit from the Old Testament quotation (4:10)?

Psalm 91:11 ____________________

42. Why do we need to look out for the use the devil's agents make of Scripture?

II Corinthians 11:14,15 ____________________

43. To what did the threefold temptation appeal?

I John 2:16 ____________________

44. When we are tempted, what has God promised to do?

I Corinthians 10:13 ____________________

The presentation of Jesus 4:14-30

Before beginning His public ministry, our Lord went back to Nazareth and showed that He was the fulfillment of Old Testament prophecy.

45. What phrase did Jesus omit in His reading of the Old Testament prophecy (4:18, 19)?

Isaiah 61:1, 2 ____________________

46. When will the latter part of the prophecy be fulfilled?

II THESSALONIANS 1:7, 8 ____________________

47. Why did Jesus not do some things in His own section of the country that He did elsewhere (4:23, 24)?

MATTHEW 13:57, 58 ____________________

48. Describe the action of these people.

4:28, 30 ____________________

49. What was the real trouble with these people?

JOHN 8:37 ____________________

50. What promise may the man of God claim under similar circumstances?

PSALM 37:32-34____________________

check-up time No. 2

You have just studied some important truths about the presentation of Christ. Now take this test to see how well you understand important truths you have studied.

Circle the letter of the correct or most nearly correct answer.

1. John the Baptist preached (a) reformation, (b) repentance, (c) forgiveness.

2. The multitude was called a generation of vipers by (a) John, (b) Judas, (c) Peter.

3. Spiritual fruit is wrought by the power of (a) Christians, (b) Satan, (c) Holy Spirit.

4. Believers are placed into the body of Christ by the Spirit's (a) baptism, (b) filling, (c) indwelling.

5. Jesus was baptized for (a) His testing, (b) identification with sinners, (c) a sign of His salvation.

6. The first man in the ancestry of Christ was (a) Abraham, (b) David, (c) Adam.

7. When He was tempted, Christ (a) used Scripture, (b) used a sword, (c) disappeared.

8. If Christ had but worshiped Satan, He would have then received (a) wealth, (b) the world, (c) wisdom.

9. Eventually, Satan will (a) be in hell, (b) be saved, (c) reign with Christ.

10. In Nazareth, Jesus (a) was anointed, (b) was stoned, (c) disappeared.

Turn to page 96 and check your answers.

LESSON 3

The Authority of Christ

4:31—6:49

Having identified Himself with man by His birth, baptism, and testing, Christ now shows His deity by His authority over every realm of nature.

Authority over demons 4:31-37

1. Give the reason the people were astonished at Christ's doctrine or teaching.

4:32 ______________________________

This verse may be translated, "And they were astonished at his teaching; for his word was with authority" (American Standard Version). Christ taught with authority because He was an authority—He was God Himself. This fact He then demonstrates.

2. How may Christ's representatives still give out the Word with power?

I CORINTHIANS 2:4, 5 ______________________________

3. What are the gospel weapons still able to do?

II CORINTHIANS 10:4, 5 ______________________________

4. Who did the demon-possessed man know Christ to be?

4:34 ______________________________

5. How did he know so much about Jesus?

JAMES 2:19 ______________________________

6. What did this miracle show about the word of Christ?

4:36 ____

7. Who to this day can deliver those who are held in bondage by spirits?

I Peter 3:22 ____

Authority over sickness 4:38-41

8. Give the reason for sickness in some Christian homes (4:38).

John 11:4 ____

9. If the Lord does not choose to be glorified in the recovery of the sick, how would He be glorified?

II Corinthians 12:9 ____

10. Which apostle evidently was married?

4:38; compare I Corinthians 9:5 ____

11. What should one surely do who has been healed (4:39)?

Psalm 116:12-14 ____

Authority to preach 4:42-44

12. Why did Christ feel He should preach in other cities also?

4:43 ____

13. Of whom should we all be thinking, after having experienced salvation ourselves?

Romans 10:14 ____

Authority over nature 5:1-11

14. What attracted people to Christ?

5:1 ____

15. Give the reason why Jesus wanted the boat (5:3).

MATTHEW 13:2, 3 ________________________________

16. What will always be the result if we will venture out in faith when Jesus speaks (5:5)?

JOHN 11:40 ________________________________

17. Give the result of laboring when not led by the Lord.

5:5; compare PSALM 127:1 ________________________________

18. Give the result of the disciples' labor when led by the Lord.

5:6 ________________________________

19. What is the promise when we labor in obedience to Christ?

I CORINTHIANS 15:58 ________________________________

20. Compare Peter's action here (5:8) with that on another occasion when Jesus gave the disciples a big catch.

JOHN 21:7 ________________________________

21. Describe the disciples' action when they reached shore.

5:11 ________________________________

22. If we have had a real vision of Christ, how will we regard the gains of this world?

PHILIPPIANS 3:7, 8 ________________________________

Authority in cleansing 5:12-16

23. How would all Jews regard this poor leper (5:12)?

LEVITICUS 13:15 ________________________________

24. What reason did Jesus have for asking some not to give publicity to his miracles (5:14)?

MARK 1:45 ________________________________

Authority over disease 5:17-26

25. How many men assisted in getting the paralyzed man to Jesus (5:18)?

MARK 2:3 ______________________________

26. Why was there such a multitude (5:19)?

5:15 ______________________________

27. What was it that Jesus saw?

5:20 ______________________________

28. How can faith be seen?

JAMES 2:18 ______________________________

29. Who were the real blasphemers (5:21)?

JAMES 2:7 ______________________________

30. If Jesus could cure a paralytic, what did it prove as to His divine authority (5:25)?

JOHN 5:36 ______________________________

31. In what way did the work of Jesus resemble the work of God in creation (5:25)?

PSALM 33:9 ______________________________

Authority over men 5:27-29

32. What will we have to do if we truly follow Jesus (5:27)?

MATTHEW 16:24 ______________________________

33. What motive should Christians have in going among people of bad repute (5:29)?

I CORINTHIANS 9:19 ______________________________

34. What was evidently Levi's motive in giving a feast?

5:31 ______________________________

Authority over tradition 5:30-39

35. Why did Jesus not call the righteous (5:32)?

ROMANS 3:10 ______

36. What did John the Baptist and his disciples do when Jesus came on the scene (5:34)?

JOHN 3:29 ______

Jesus was showing the scribes and Pharisees that John and his disciples were hoping for the presence of Christ. He also told them that since law and grace are diverse principles, men should not try to pour the gospel wine into the old wineskins of the law (5:37, 38; GALATIANS 5:1, 18; COLOSSIANS 2:20).

Authority over the Sabbath 6:1-5

37. What was the law they thought Jesus was violating (6:2)?

EXODUS 31:15 ______

38. For whom was the Sabbath made?

MARK 2:27 ______

Authority over deformity 6:6-11

39. What are the enemies of God always trying to do?

6:7; compare PSALM 37:32; 38:12; JEREMIAH 20:10 ______

______

40. Describe the condition of the restored hand.

6:10 ______

41. What prophecy did these religious rulers fulfill by getting angry (6:11)?

PSALM 2:2 ______

Authority over the twelve 6:12-49

42. Describe the action of Christ before He chose the twelve.

6:12 ________________________________

43. What will be the sure result of going into service through His call (6:13)?

John 15:16 ________________________________

44. When is it a blessing to be poor?

6:20; compare James 2:5 ________________________

45. Why may Christians expect to be persecuted?

6:22; compare John 15:19, 20 ______________________

46. What is the best way to treat our enemies?

6:27; compare Romans 12:20 ______________________

47. Why should Christians do good to others even when it is not gratefully received?

6:35; compare I Peter 2:20 ______________________

48. What do such actions prove to the world?

Romans 5:5 ______________________________

49. Who is the one to do the judging (6:37)?

Romans 14:4, 12 ____________________________

50. When we give according to 6:38, what do we gain aside from a temporary blessing?

Matthew 6:19, 20 ____________________________

51. To whom was Jesus referring indirectly in speaking of blind leaders (6:39)?

Matthew 23:16; compare Isaiah 9:16 __________________

52. Whose life and work are always in need of careful examination?

6:41, 42; compare GALATIANS 6:4 ______

53. If one has Christ in his heart, what will be true of his mouth?

6:45; compare PROVERBS 16:23 ______

54. How many nationalities are to be taught to observe the teachings of Christ in this age?

6:47; compare MATTHEW 28:19 ______

55. Who shows that he loves Christ the most?

JOHN 14:21 ______

56. For how long will the Christ-rejecter be able to withstand the vehement winds of trial (6:49)?

PROVERBS 28:18 ______

check-up time No. 3

You have just studied some important truths about the authority of Christ. Review your study by rereading the questions and your written answers. If you wish, you may use the self-check test as an aid in reviewing your lesson. If you aren't sure of an answer, reread the Scripture portion given to see if you can find the answer. Then take this test to see how well you understand important truths you have studied.

In the right-hand margin write "True" or "False" after each of the following statements.

1. Christ taught with authority because He was an authority. ____T____
2. Demons believe there is a God. ____T____
3. The sickness of some Christians is for God's glory. ____T____
4. All that attracted people to Christ was His physical healing. ____F____
5. The disciples caught nothing when they were led of the Lord. ____F____
6. In following Christ, the disciples forsook all. ____T____
7. The purpose of Christ was to call the righteous to repentance. ____F____
8. Before Christ chose His disciples, He prayed all night. ____T____
9. The believer is to judge other Christians. ____F____
10. The Christ-rejecter will be able to stand the winds of trial. ____F____

Turn to page 96 and check your answers.

LESSON 4

The Ministry of Christ

7:1—9:50

Having shown the authority of Christ over men and nature, the Gospel writer now shows the ministry of Christ.

Ministry in sickness 7:1-10

1. What kind of servant had the sick man evidently been (7:2)?

COLOSSIANS 3:22, 23 ____________________

2. Describe what the centurion thought about his worthiness.

7:6, 7 ____________________

3. What is one of the great conditions of prevailing prayer?

PSALM 10:17 ____________________

4. What kind of estimate did the centurion evidently have of Jesus?

7:7, 8; compare PSALM 33:9 ____________________

5. Why is it remarkable that Christ had not found such faith in Israel (7:9)?

PSALM 147:19, 20 ____________________

6. At what time had the cure taken place (7:10)?

MATTHEW 8:13 ____________________

Ministry in death 7:11-17

7. How did Jesus feel when He witnessed sorrow and affliction in others?

7:13; compare Isaiah 63:9 ______________________________

8. Who is some day going to wipe away all our tears forever?

Revelation 21:4 ______________________________

9. What did Jesus' ability to raise the dead prove (7:15)?

John 5:21 ______________________________

10. Give the results that proved this man was alive again.

7:15 ______________________________

11. Who else did Jesus raise from the dead?

8:54, 55; John 11:43, 44 ______________________________

12. What had the people evidently learned about Jesus?

7:16; compare Matthew 1:23 ______________________________

Ministry in doubt 7:18-35

13. What was the question of John the Baptist?

7:19 ______________________________

14. What reason did John have for thinking that Jesus was the Promised One?

John 1:33, 34 ______________________________

15. What was the greatest witness for Jesus?

7:22; compare John 5:36; 14:11 ______________________________

16. What did John's manner of dress testify as to his character (7:25)?

Isaiah 59:17 ______________________________

17. In what important relation to the dispensations did John stand?

16:16 ____

18. What did John say of himself (7:27)?

John 1:22, 23 ____

19. Describe the character of the Pharisees and lawyers.

7:30; compare Jeremiah 8:8 ______________________________

20. What did the sulky and obstinate spirit of the Pharisees and lawyers prove about them (7:31, 32)?

Jeremiah 5:4 ____

21. How did these leaders describe Christ?

7:34; John 8:48 ____

22. Why could not these leaders endorse the spiritual truths of Christ?

I Corinthians 2:14 ______________________________

Ministry to sinners 7:36-50

23. Why did some social leaders murmur against Christ (7:36)?

19:7 ____

24. Give the reason Christ came into the world.

19:10 ____

25. What spirit especially pleases our Lord?

Psalm 51:17 Holy Spirit ____

26. Compare the manifested adoration of this woman with that of the humility of Christ.

7:38; compare John 13:4, 5 ______________________________

27. What is the Lord's opinion of those who take the "more holy than thou" attitude (7:39)?

ISAIAH 65:5 ______________________________

28. Who alone can pay our debt to God (7:42)?

ROMANS 5:6; GALATIANS 3:13; EPHESIANS 1:7 ______________

29. What should we all do when our bonds have been loosed?

PSALM 116:16-18 ______________________________

30. What did the actions of the woman demonstrate?

7:47 ______________________________

31. What kind of love does Jesus want?

I JOHN 3:18 ______________________________

32. What saved this woman's soul?

7:50 ______________________________

Ministry of women 8:1-3

33. What was the particular ministry of these women?

8:3 ______________________________

Ministry of the Word of God 8:4-21

34. What does the seed stand for (8:5)?

8:11 ______________________________

35. Who are the wayside hearers (8:5)?

8:12 ______________________________

36. Who is represented by the fowls (8:5)?

8:12 ______________________________

37. What does the hardened soil upon which the seed fell represent?

8:12 ______________________________

38. Who are the rocky ground hearers (8:6)?

8:13 ______________________________

39. What do the thorns represent (8:7)?

8:14 ______________________________

40. What is shown about those who are in love with the pleasures of this world?

I John 2:15 ______________________________

41. Who are the good ground hearers (8:8)?

8:15 ______________________________

42. How can a person get a good heart?

Psalm 51:10 ______________________________

43. What was the result of Israel's willful attitude toward Christ's teaching (8:10)?

Romans 11:7, 8 ______________________________

44. Why is the Christian's light to be set on a candlestick (8:16)?

II Corinthians 3:2 ______________________________

45. Who are the nearest "relatives" that Jesus has?

8:21; compare I John 2:5; Hebrews 2:11 ______________________________

Ministry of faith 8:22-25

46. What assurance should the disciples have had that they were not going to sink?

8:22 ______________________________

47. When we feel ourselves sinking, what is the wise thing to do?

Psalm 69:1, 2; 116:3, 4 ______________________________

Ministry among the demon possessed 8:26-39

48. Describe the violence of this demon-possessed man.

8:29: compare MATTHEW 8:28 ______________________________

49. How did the man recognize Jesus as the Son of God (8:28)?

JAMES 2:19 ______________________________

50. Why did the devils fear the deep or abyss (8:31)?

REVELATION 20:1-3 ______________________________

51. Why were the keepers of the hogs stirred up about the matter (8:34)?

JOB 21:13-15 ______________________________

52. When the Lord has done a great thing for us, how should we feel?

8:39; compare PSALM 126:3 ______________________________

Ministry in sickness and death 8:40-56

53. Describe Jairus' earthly position in life.

8:41 ______________________________

54. To what may the woman's touch for healing be compared (8:44)?

ROMANS 4:5 ______________________________

55. What exhortation does the Christian have concerning wailing about those whose bodies are asleep until the resurrection (8:52)?

I THESSALONIANS 4:13 ______________________________

The ministry of the twelve 9:1-9

56. Who gave the disciples power over demons and diseases?

9:1 ______________________________

57. Why did the power of healing accompany the preaching of the gospel in the days before the New Testament was written (9:2)?

HEBREWS 2:3, 4 ______________________________

The ministry to the five thousand 9:10-17

58. What did Jesus put before healing?

9:11; compare ISAIAH 61:1 ______________________________

59. Who in the crowd had the loaves and fishes (9:13)?

JOHN 6:9 ______________________________

60. What is God able to do with the seemingly insignificant things if they are yielded to His hands?

I CORINTHIANS 1:27, 28 ______________________________

61. What will always be true of those who feed upon the Bread of Life (9:17)?

PROVERBS 13:25; JOHN 6:35 ______________________________

The ministry in revelation 9:18-50

62. Who revealed to Peter that Jesus was more than a man (9:20)?

MATTHEW 16:17 ______________________________

63. Of what events was Christ speaking?

9:22; compare I CORINTHIANS 15:3, 4 ______________________________

64. How is it that one who loses his life for Christ's sake can gain it (9:24)?

JOHN 12:26 ______________________________

65. Why should a Christian speak out boldly for Christ in the world (9:26)?

ROMANS 1:16 ______________________________

66. Who did not taste death until they had a foretaste of the kingdom of God (9:27-36)?

II PETER 1:16-18 ______________________________

67. How long was it before they saw this kingdom?

9:28 ______________________________

Unredeemed man cannot bear to see the full blaze of the glory of God (EXODUS 33:23). Thus, the glory of Christ had to be veiled for Him to descend to earth. At His transfiguration this veil was lifted for an instant.

68. Who were the disciples to hear instead of Peter?

9:35 ______________________________

69. Who was meant by the perverse generation (9:41)?

MATTHEW 12:39; 16:4 ______________________________

70. What prediction did Christ again make?

9:44 ______________________________

71. How long was it before they perceived these things (9:45)?

24:44, 45 ______________________________

check-up time No. 4

You have just studied some important truths about the ministry of Christ. Now take this test to see how well you understand important truths you have studied.

Circle the letter of the correct or most nearly correct answer.

1. The centurion instructed his servants to tell Christ he was (a) worthy, (b) unworthy, (c) working.

2. When Christ raised the widow's son, the people (a) were angry, (b) stoned Him, (c) glorified God.

3. The greatest witness for Jesus was (a) John, (b) the Pharisees, (c) miracles.

4. The woman who anointed Jesus' feet was saved by her (a) faith, (b) adoration, (c) works.

5. In the parable of the sower, the seed stands for (a) the hearers, (b) the Word, (c) the devil.

6. In the parable of the sower, the fowls represent (a) the hearers, (b) the Word, (c) the devil.

7. The demon-possessed man was (a) wise, (b) wild, (c) wealthy.

8. Jairus was (a) a ruler, (b) rich, (c) rebellious.

9. The number of baskets left over after feeding the five thousand were as many as (a) the people, (b) the disciples, (c) the loaves and fishes.

10. On the mount of transfiguration, the disciples were to hear (a) Christ instead of Peter, (b) Moses instead of Elijah, (c) Peter instead of Christ.

Turn to page 96 and check your answers.

LESSON 5

The Rejection of Christ

9:51—11:54

Although the conclusion of Christ's rejection was His crucifixion, the progress of His rejection is presented in this section. Our Lord had shown His authority and ministry, and now this was rejected.

The rejection in Samaria 9:51-56

1. Where was Christ determined to go?

9:51 ______________________________

2. How may we imitate Christ in this?

PHILIPPIANS 3:14 ______________________________

3. Where did the disciples get the idea of calling down fire (9:54)?

II KINGS 1:10, 12 ______________________________

4. When Jesus rebukes one, what does it prove (9:55)?

REVELATION 3:19 ______________________________

5. How should we rebuke a sinning brother?

17:3 ______________________________

6. What does God's desire to save cause Him to do?

II PETER 3:15 ______________________________

The rejection of Christ's call 9:57-62

7. What did Jesus discern to be the trouble with this man (9:57)?

14:28-33 ______________________________

8. Who was this man (9:57)?

MATTHEW 8:19 ______________________________

In verse 59, the idea of remaining home to bury his father was the customary way of saying, "I don't want to leave home until after my father dies." It does not imply that the father was then a corpse.

9. What class of "dead" people did Jesus probably imply would care for the aged father?

EPHESIANS 2:5; I TIMOTHY 5:6 ______________________________

10. What resulted from Mark's longing glances toward home (9:62)?

ACTS 15:37, 38 ______________________________

The ministry of the seventy 10:1-24

11. What is our first responsibility in light of the great harvest?

10:2 ______________________________

12. Why should we ask the Lord to send forth workers?

JEREMIAH 3:15 ______________________________

13. What advice does a Christian worker need when going out among wolves (10:3)?

MATTHEW 10:16 ______________________________

14. Why may we expect to run up against wolves in the Lord's service?

JOHN 15:20 ______________________________

15. Why would there be no need of carrying money or provisions (10:4)?

GENESIS 24:33, 56; I SAMUEL 21:8; LUKE 22:35 ____________

16. What ministry is given to us all?

II CORINTHIANS 5:18-20 ____________

17. What does the gospel bring into the home (10:5)?

EPHESIANS 2:17 ____________

18. How near does the kingdom of God get to some people (10:11)?

ROMANS 10:18, 21 ____________

19. What will make it less tolerable for those who reject Christ (10:12)?

JOHN 3:19 ____________

20. Why is it that one who hears the servant of Christ is actually hearing the Lord (10:16)?

I THESSALONIANS 4:8 ____________

21. When did Jesus see Satan cast out of his original position (10:18)?

ISAIAH 14:12-19 ____________

22. Where are some people's names written?

10:20 ____________

23. What has God pronounced upon those who are so intellectual in their own estimation that they cannot accept His terms (10:21)?

ISAIAH 5:21 ____________

24. Whom does God often use to stop the mouths of enemies of the gospel?

PSALM 8:2 ____________

25. Why should we consider it a great privilege to have spiritual sight?

10:24; compare MATTHEW 13:17 ______________________________

26. Who else would like to have a personal understanding of some of the blessed truths known only to redeemed men?

I PETER 1:12 ______________________________

The rejection by the lawyer 10:25-37

27. What did the lawyer want to know?

10:25 ______________________________

28. What answer was given another man that asked this same question?

ACTS 16:31 ______________________________

29. Why did Jesus send this particular lawyer to the law (10:26)?

ROMANS 3:19, 20 ______________________________

30. What did he need more than a knowledge of law?

JOHN 1:17; 14:6 ______________________________

31. What word sums up the law of God?

ROMANS 13:8-10; JAMES 2:8 ______________________________

32. How does the law show that God's love was not in his heart?

10:29 ______________________________

33. What was the relationship of the Jews to the Samaritans (10:33)?

JOHN 4:9 ______________________________

34. Why is it worthwhile to do deeds of this kind (10:34, 35)?

PROVERBS 19:17 ______________________________

35. What is required of Christians (10:37)?

MICAH 6:8 ______________________________

Reception amidst rejection 10:38-42

36. Where was Mary sitting?

10:39 ______

37. What does the Bible say about the person who waits quietly before Him?

PROVERBS 8:34 ______

38. What is the effect of becoming cumbered with the cares of life (10:40)?

MARK 4:19 ______

39. With whom should we be concerned, rather than with the cares of this life (10:41)?

HEBREWS 12:2 ______

40. What one thing should we desire of the Lord (10:42)?

PSALM 27:4 ______

Instruction in prayer 11:1-13

41. Why do we need to be taught to pray (11:1)?

ROMANS 8:26 ______

42. Under whose guidance should we always seek to pray?

EPHESIANS 6:18; JUDE 20 ______

43. Who alone can call God "Father" (11:2)?

GALATIANS 3:26 ______

44. When we pray "Thy kingdom come," what other coming is involved (11:2)?

REVELATION 22:20 ______

45. What happens when a Christian sins (11:4)?

Ephesians 4:30 ____________________

46. Why do we need to come to God when we are tempted?

I Corinthians 10:13 ____________________

47. What conditions are placed upon the command to ask (11:9)?

John 15:7; I John 3:22; Matthew 21:22 ____________________

Rejection by Israel 11:14-36

48. What argument silenced the charge that Jesus cast out Satanic powers by Satanic power?

11:17, 18 ____________________

49. What does the "finger of God" stand for?

Exodus 8:19 ____________________

50. Why is one counted against Christ who is not with Him (11:23)?

Matthew 6:24 ____________________

51. What did the house need, aside from being swept and garnished, if the evil spirits were to be kept out (11:25)?

Ephesians 5:18; I Corinthians 3:16 ____________________

52. What was the sign of Jonas (11:29)?

Matthew 12:40 ____________________

53. Who was the queen of the south (11:31)?

I Kings 10:1, 2 ____________________

54. If people would repent at the words of a frail mortal like Jonah, what greater reason for repenting did they then have?

11:32; compare Hebrews 7:26 ____________________

Result of rejection 11:37-54

55. What was the real trouble with these men?

11:39; compare II Timothy 3:5 ______________________________

The tombstones (11:44) were whitewashed yearly to make them easily discernible, it being considered defiling to step on a grave.

56. What does this imply about the Pharisees (11:44)?

Psalm 5:9; Hosea 9:8 ______________________________

57. Describe the rejection these men showed for Christ.

11:52 ______________________________

check-up time No. 5

You have just studied some important truths about the rejection of Christ. Review your study by rereading the questions and your written answers. If you wish, you may use the self-check test as an aid in reviewing your lesson. If you aren't sure of an answer, reread the Scripture portion given to see if you can find the answer. Then take this test to see how well you understand important truths you have studied.

In the right-hand margin write "True" or "False" after each of the following statements.

1. Christ had come to destroy the lives of men. F
2. In following Christ, we must give Him first place. T
3. Our first responsibility in the harvest of souls is to send forth laborers. F
4. All Christians have the ministry of reconciliation. T
5. Angels desire to have a personal understanding of spiritual truth. T
6. The way to gain eternal life is to keep the Mosaic law. F
7. The Jews highly respected the Samaritans. F
8. Mary sat at the feet of Jesus and heard His word. T
9. Christ was accused of working miracles by the power of Satan. T
10. The leaders of Israel encouraged others to accept Christ. F

Turn to page 96 and check your answers.

Lesson 6

The Warnings of Christ

12:1—13:35

In the chapters before the triumphal entry (Luke 19), Christ gives instruction in the light of His rejection. He warns His people as well as sinners in this lesson.

The warning of hypocrisy 12:1-12

1. What does leaven stand for aside from hypocrisy (12:1)?

Matthew 16:11, 12 ____________________

2. How had Jesus already referred to the hypocrisy of the Pharisees?

11:39 ____________________

3. When will that which is covered be revealed (12:2)?

I Corinthians 4:5 ____________________

4. Who is around when men are planning things in the dark (12:3)?

Psalm 94:9 ____________________

5. Why can no serious harm come to Christ's friends (12:4)?

Philippians 1:28 ____________________

6. If God is thoughtful of such insignificant things as sparrows (12:6), what should believers always be encouraged to do?

I Peter 5:7; Psalm 50:11, 15 ____________________

7. What class only does Jesus represent before the Father (12:8)?

John 17:8, 9 ______________________________

8. What was it that Jesus defined as blaspheming the Holy Ghost (12:10)?

Matthew 12:24, 32 ______________________________

The unpardonable sin was ascribing Christ's works while on earth wrought by the Holy Spirit to the power of Satan. Since Christ has ascended, the only unpardonable sin is that of unbelief (John 16:9). Certainly whosoever will may come (John 6:37, 44).

9. Why should those being publicly persecuted for Christ's sake leave it to the Holy Spirit to prompt them as to what to say (12:12)?

21:13-15 ______________________________

The warning of covetousness 12:13-34

10. What did Jesus detect was behind the man's request?

12:15 ______________________________

11. Of what serious sin did Jesus evidently think this man was guilty?

Ephesians 5:5, 6 ______________________________

12. If men do not use their God-given prosperity for His glory, what will happen (12:16)?

Hosea 2:8-11 ______________________________

13. What is the right way to lay up treasure (12:18)?

Mark 10:21 ______________________________

14. What would all the riches in the world fail to buy (12:19)?

Psalm 52:5-7 ______________________________

15. Why is a man a fool to put off his salvation?

12:20; compare Psalm 78:30, 31 ______________________________

16. What does it mean to be without anxious thought (12:22)?

HEBREWS 13:5 ______________________________

17. What are we therefore to do?

12:31 ______________________________

18. What is the lesson of verse 24?

PHILIPPIANS 4:19 ______________________________

19. If God provides so wonderfully for the things of His creation which are not able to work, what may one expect who is able to help himself?

12:28; compare PSALM 84:11 ______________________________

20. What did God do for Solomon because he put first things first (12:31)?

I KINGS 3:11-13 ______________________________

21. What is the real way to get rich?

12:33; compare I TIMOTHY 6:18, 19 ______________________________

22. Where is the Christian's heart supposed to be located?

12:34; compare COLOSSIANS 3:1, 3 ______________________________

The warnings of the second coming 12:35-59

23. What is the Christian's light (12:35)?

JOHN 1:8, 9 ______________________________

24. What is ever to be the blessed hope of the Church (12:36)?

TITUS 2:13 ______________________________

25. How will Christ's coming take the world?

12:39; compare I THESSALONIANS 5:2, 3 ______________________________

26. To whom especially does the warning of stewardship apply (12:43)?

I TIMOTHY 5:17 ______________________________

27. Describe the effect of the hope of Christ's coming.

I John 3:3 ______

28. Give the thinking of an unfaithful servant.

12:45 ______

29. What does opportunity have to do with responsibility (12:47)?

Matthew 11:21-24 ______

30. How may the degree of sin be increased?

John 9:41 ______

31. To what did this baptism refer (12:50)?

Matthew 20:18, 22 ______

32. When did the division in families on the religious question begin (12:52, 53)?

Genesis 4:4, 5 ______

33. Why does the dividing line still run through families?

John 15:19-21 ______

34. Who only was able to discern the times (12:56)?

Matthew 11:25 ______

35. Since the Jewish nation at that very moment was on the way to judgment, what should they have done (12:58)?

Isaiah 55:6 ______

36. What words will every Christ-rejecter hear?

Matthew 25:41 ______

The warning of repentance 13:1-9

37. What was to be the fate of the Jewish people if they did not repent?

13:5; compare 19:43, 44; 21:24 ______

38. Who is represented by the fig tree planted in the vineyard (13:6, 7)?

PSALM 80:8-16; ISAIAH 5:1-4 ______________________________

39. What did the Jews do, even when extraordinary forbearance was shown to them?

ROMANS 2:4 ______________________________

40. What is meant by the trees being cut down (13:9)?

ROMANS 11:8-10 ______________________________

The teaching of Israel's need 13:10-17

41. Who alone is able to heal by a word?

13:12; compare PSALM 107:20 ______________________________

42. What did the Jewish leaders say about Jesus for doing good on the Sabbath (13:14)?

JOHN 9:16 ______________________________

43. What attitude will all who have been against Christ, eventually come to?

13:17; compare ISAIAH 45:24 ______________________________

The teaching of the kingdom program 13:18-21

44. What figure did Daniel use to portray a mighty kingdom that gave temporary shelter to nations and yet proved insecure (13:19)?

DANIEL 4:19-24 ______________________________

45. How did Christ interpret leaven (13:21)?

MATTHEW 16:6; MARK 8:15 ______________________________

46. Since meal is never used in an evil sense, and is typical of spiritual food, who must this woman be who is engaged in a forbidden action—mixing leaven in meal?

REVELATION 17:1-6 ____________________

47. When will the whole be leavened?

MATTHEW 24:21-26 ____________________

The warnings on the way to Jerusalem 13:22-35

48. What was more important than knowing how many would be saved?

13:24 ____________________

49. When, in the future, will the door of the strait gate be shut (13:25)?

MATTHEW 25:10 ____________________

50. What class can never hear the words, "I know you not" (13:27)?

I CORINTHIANS 8:3; II TIMOTHY 2:19 ____________________

51. On what basis did Abraham, Isaac, and Jacob attain this kingdom (13:28)?

HEBREWS 11:8, 20, 21 ____________________

52. Where had Jesus prophesied He would be crucified (13:33)?

MATTHEW 20:18 ____________________

53. Who has been gathered under His wings (13:34)?

PSALM 91:1-4 ____________________

54. How did Jesus later make clear what He meant by leaving their house desolate (13:35)?

21:5, 6, 24 ____________________

55. When will the day come when Israel will call Him blessed?

REVELATION 1:7; MATTHEW 24:30-31 ____________________

check-up time No. 6

You have just studied some important truths about the warnings of Christ. Now take this test to see how well you understand important truths you have studied.

Circle the letter of the correct or most nearly correct answer.

1. Jesus denounced the Pharisees as (a) brigands, (b) adulterers, (c) hypocrites.

2. Ascribing Christ's works while here on earth to the power of Satan instead of the Holy Spirit was (a) not blaspheming, (b) unpardonable, (c) forgiven.

3. We are to seek (a) the kingdom of God, (b) things we possess, (c) treasure that corrupts.

4. Christ rebuked the disciples' lack of faith by reminding them how God provided for (a) the angels, (b) the grass, (c) Solomon.

5. The Christian's heart is to be set on things (a) below, (b) he possesses, (c) above.

6. The blessed hope of the Church is (a) the appearing of Christ, (b) the appearing of the tribulation, (c) the appearing of the millennium.

7. All who reject Christ will be (a) in heaven, (b) in hell, (c) annihilated.

8. The fig tree represents (a) Christians, (b) Gentiles, (c) Israel.

9. Daniel portrays a mighty kingdom that proved insecure as (a) a seed, (b) a leaf, (c) a tree.

10. Abraham, Isaac, and Jacob obtained the kingdom by (a) faith, (b) birth, (c) works.

Turn to page 96 and check your answers.

LESSON 7

The Parables of Christ

14:1—15:32

Christ used many parables to teach important spiritual truths. In these chapters He teaches by parables in view of His rejection. A parable is a short story from which a spiritual truth is drawn.

Parables in the Pharisee's house 14:1-24

1. What use did Jesus make of social gatherings (14:1)?

5:29; 7:36; 11:37 ______________________________

2. Why did Jesus answer the lawyers and Pharisees when they had asked Him nothing (14:3)?

MATTHEW 9:4 ______________________________

3. Where else did these men seize the best seats (14:7)?

11:43 ______________________________

4. What is the correct spirit to show on such occasions?

PHILIPPIANS 2:3 ______________________________

5. What will come upon those who try to promote themselves (14:9)?

PROVERBS 3:35 ______________________________

6. Why are some not bidden higher in the Lord's service (14:10)?

PROVERBS 15:33 ______________________________

7. Whom does the Lord delight to put in places of great service (14:11)?

I SAMUEL 15:17 ______

8. When a person is seeking exaltation, what does it indicate about his attitude toward the Lord?

PSALM 138:6 ______

9. What unjust condition exists in human society (14:13)?

PROVERBS 14:20 ______

10. When we lend to the Lord, what do we get on the investment (14:14)?

PROVERBS 19:17 ______

11. To what time does verse 15 evidently look forward?

REVELATION 19:9 ______

12. Who were those originally bidden to the great gospel feast (14:16)?

MATTHEW 10:5, 6 ______

13. What is the invitation that was sent out (14:17)?

II CORINTHIANS 5:19, 20 ______

14. What is a frequent result of the possession of property (14:18)?

8:14; 18:23, 24; II TIMOTHY 4:4, 10 ______

15. What was the real trouble with this person who put up such a foolish excuse (14:19)?

II CORINTHIANS 4:4; JEREMIAH 17:9 ______

16. Who has first claim on a Christian's affection?

14:26 ______

17. To what particular company that was quickly called, does verse 22 probably refer?

ACTS 2:38, 39 ______

18. To whom does this third invitation, which followed Pentecost, probably refer (14:23)?

ROMANS 11:11; MATTHEW 12:18; MARK 16:15, 16 ______________

19. What is meant by compelling men?

II CORINTHIANS 5:11, 20; 6:1 ______________

20. How wide is the invitation now?

REVELATION 22:17 ______________

21. What happened to those who during Christ's mission on earth rejected Him (14:24)?

MATTHEW 21:43 ______________

Parables of discipleship 14:25-35

22. What is the meaning of the precept in verse 26?

MATTHEW 10:37; PHILIPPIANS 3:7, 8 ______________

23. What is the true way to look upon our lives?

ACTS 20:24 ______________

24. What does cross-bearing imply (14:27)?

14:33 ______________

25. If we have fellowship with Christ in His suffering, of what may we be assured?

PHILIPPIANS 3:10, 11; II TIMOTHY 1:12 ______________

26. When a person has truly received Christ's salvation, who will look after the finishing process (14:30)?

PHILIPPIANS 1:6 ______________

27. How do the world's rulers show their wisdom in preparing for war?

14:31, 32; compare PROVERBS 20:18 ______________

28. Who is supposed to be the permeating and seasoning influence for God in the world (14:34)?

MATTHEW 5:13 ______________________________

Parable of the lost sheep 15:1-7

29. What special points did Jesus make in the succeeding parables for the benefit of these Pharisees and scribes?

15:7, 10, 25-28 ______________________________

30. Why was their argument against His receiving sinners weak (15:2)?

MATTHEW 9:12 ______________________________

31. What sheep were lost in a special sense (15:4)?

MATTHEW 10:6 ______________________________

32. How many others were as lost sheep?

ISAIAH 53:6 ______________________________

33. Who was the good shepherd?

JOHN 10:11 ______________________________

34. What does the bearing of the lamb upon His shoulders suggest (15:5)?
ISAIAH 63:9; I PETER 1:5 ______________________________

35. When once the sheep is in His grasp, who is responsible for its keeping?

JOHN 10:28, 29 ______________________________

36. What class is probably referred to in the mention of those who "need no repentance" (15:7)?

16:14, 15 ______________________________

37. Why did they really need to repent?

PROVERBS 30:12 ______________________________

Parable of the lost silver 15:8-10

38. What is a good candle to carry in looking for the lost (15:8)?

PSALM 119:105 ______

39. Since a coin cannot well return of itself, how is it like many lost sinners?

14:23 ______

40. Besides Christians, who else takes an interest in the salvation of souls?

15:10; compare HEBREWS 1:14 ______

Parable of the lost sons 15:11-32

41. What is the best portion of goods for us to have (15:12)?

PSALM 16:5, 6 ______

42. Compare this description with Israel (15:13).

JEREMIAH 2:5, 13 ______

43. Who is a near relative of the man who wastes his substance?

PROVERBS 18:9 ______

44. What does love of the world's pleasure always lead to in time?

15:14; compare PROVERBS 21:17 ______

45. What is God's attitude toward one who deliberately chooses to run the gauntlet of sin?

ROMANS 1:24 ______

46. How low down will sin bring a person?

15:16; compare PSALM 73:22 ______

47. When a sinner comes to himself, how does he feel (15:17)?

JEREMIAH 31:19 ______

48. When a man is ready to arise, what is God ready to do (15:18)?

EZEKIEL 18:28; PSALM 116:3-5 ______________________________

49. How should men therefore look upon their sins?

PSALM 25:11 ______________________________

50. Who does God think is worthy (15:19)?

18:13, 14 A Servant ______________________________

51. Of what does the father's running to meet his son speak (15:20)?

ROMANS 3:24; 5:8; EPHESIANS 2:8 ______________________________

52. What does the eating and making merry signify (15:23)?

15:10 ______________________________

53. Who failed to join in Christ's longing to save the lost (15:25, 26)?

15:2 ______________________________

54. Seeing the elder son had done nothing more than his duty, what should he have considered himself (15:29)?

17:10 ______________________________

55. What opinion did the elder son evidently have of himself (15:30)?

18:11, 12 ______________________________

56. Who especially should be filled with gladness at being found (15:32)?

ROMANS 15:9-15 ______________________________

57. Why was it fitting that they should make merry?

EPHESIANS 2:1-7 ______________________________

check-up time No. 7

You have just studied some important truths about the parables of Christ. Review your study by rereading the questions and your written answers. If you wish, you may use the self-check test as an aid in reviewing your lesson. If you aren't sure of an answer, reread the Scripture portion to see if you can find the answer. Then take this test to see how well you understand important truths you have studied.

In the right-hand margin write "True" or "False" after each of the following statements.

1. The Lord delights to use those of a humble spirit. T
2. The possession of things often leads one away from Christ. T
3. The invited guests came quickly to the great supper. F
4. Those who bear the cross of Christ must forsake all. T
5. Leaders seldom count the cost before a war. F
6. The Lord was willing to befriend sinners because He knew their need of salvation. T
7. Christ is responsible for keeping His sheep. T
8. All sinners know they need to repent. F
9. The love of worldly pleasure brings enduring satisfaction. F
10. Men should be ashamed of their sin. T

Turn to page 96 and check your answers.

LESSON 8

The Service for Christ

16:1—17:37

Christ continues to teach in light of His rejection. He now instructs in Christian service as it relates to Israel and His second coming.

Instruction concerning wealth 16:1-31

1. How many should consider themselves stewards (16:1)?

I CORINTHIANS 4:1; I PETER 4:10 ______________________

2. How did Jesus illustrate the waster?

16:19 ______________________

3. What people were stewards in a special sense?

ROMANS 9:4, 5 ______________________

4. To what extent will men have to give account of their stewardship (16:2)?

MATTHEW 12:36 ______________________

5. What is the best answer to the question, "What shall I do" (16:3)?

15:18 ______________________

6. What had this man accomplished, both for himself and his master, by accepting the small amounts in full payment of what they owed (16:5-7)?

16:9 ______________________

Note "lord" not "Lord" in verse 8, which shows the employer, not the Lord, commended this man for this underhanded trick.

7. What class is meant by "children of this world" (16:8)?

PSALM 17:14 ______________________________

8. What incentive is there to make the opportunities of the present life count for the needs of the great eternity to follow?

14:15 ______________________________

9. Why is money referred to as "mammon of unrighteousness" (16:9)?

PROVERBS 22:16; JEREMIAH 17:11 ______________________________

10. How does a Christian prove himself a good steward?

I PETER 4:10 ______________________________

11. What parable had Jesus given as a foundation to this one?

14:13, 14 ______________________________

12. Who is a good illustration of the one who was unfaithful in handling the mammon (16:11)?

JOHN 12:4, 6; 13:2, 27 ______________________________

13. What is meant by the true riches?

12:33 ______________________________

14. Who is able at any time to recall that which a man thinks is his own (16:12)?

12:20 ______________________________

15. Give the reason a man cannot serve both God and mammon (16:13).

JAMES 4:4; I JOHN 2:15, 16 ______________________________

16. Why does human opinion bear no weight with God?

16:15; compare I SAMUEL 16:7 ______________________________

17. What class especially is looked upon by God as an abomination?

PROVERBS 16:5 ______________________________

18. When did the dispensation of grace have its beginning?

16:16; compare John 1:17 ______________________________

19. Though the planets in the heavens should fall and earth itself should be crumpled up, what is sure to stand?

16:17; compare I Peter 1:25 ______________________________

20. What exception is made for divorce in Matthew's account (16:18)?

Matthew 5:32; 19:9 ______________________________

Fornication, in the scriptural sense, is an act of impurity committed before marriage; adultery, the act after marriage. In the case of adultery, death was the punishment under the law. (See Leviticus 20:10.)

21. For how long is a couple to remain married?

Romans 7:3; I Corinthians 7:39 ______________________________

22. How do people often feel about those who fare sumptuously in this life (16:19)?

Psalm 73:3-7 ______________________________

23. What is the other side of the matter?

Psalm 73:17-20 ______________________________

24. If the righteous are temporarily afflicted, what promise have they (16:20)?

Psalm 34:19 ______________________________

25. How is Lazarus' condition described?

16:22 ______________________________

26. What is implied about the beggar, that he should be pictured as going to heaven?

Revelation 14:13 ______________________________

27. Why did the rich man wake up in hades (16:23)?

Revelation 20:14; Psalm 9:17 ______________________________

Hades is the place of lost spirits who have departed, and not the final hell.

28. When is the best time to be praying for mercy (16:24)?

Isaiah 55:6 ______________________________

29. What water could have put out the flames of desire during the rich man's lifetime?

John 4:14 ______________________________

30. What did the rich man's memory bring before him, aside from the sins of his lifetime?

16:28 ______________________________

31. When is the time to be concerned about the salvation of others?

Romans 10:1; I Corinthians 9:22; II Corinthians 5:11 ________

32. What is the real reason men will not accept God's salvation (16:31)?

II Corinthians 4:3, 4 ______________________________

33. What great resurrection from the dead was given to Jews to convince them of the truth of the gospel?

Romans 1:3, 4 ______________________________

Instruction in forgiveness 17:1-6

34. To what does the "offenses" refer (17:1)?

I Corinthians 11:19 ______________________________

35. What is the source of false teaching that causes the damnation of souls?

Galatians 5:19-21 ______________________________

36. In what spirit should the offending brother be approached (17:3)?

GALATIANS 6:1 ______________________________

37. What should always be the Christian's attitude toward one who has injured him?

ROMANS 12:21 ______________________________

38. Why is it well to look to Jesus for an increase of faith (17:5)?

HEBREWS 12:2 ______________________________

39. Who alone could give one such faith as defined in verse 6?

ROMANS 12:3 ______________________________

Instruction in service 17:7-10

40. How will the true servant always feel about the performance of duty to God (17:10)?

I CHRONICLES 29:14 ______________________________

Instruction in thankfulness 17:11-19

41. Why were the lepers afar off (17:12)?

LEVITICUS 13:45, 46 ______________________________

42. Why were the lepers to go to the priests (17:14)?

MATTHEW 8:4 ______________________________

43. What distinction had the nine Jews forgotten in their common misery?

17:16; compare JOHN 4:9 ______________________________

44. When God heals a person, what has He a right to expect?

PSALM 30:1, 2, 11, 12 ______________________________

45. For what else did Samaritans have a reputation with Jesus, aside from gratitude for blessings received?

10:32-35 ______________________________

46. What was the matter with the nine lepers?

Psalm 106:13 ______________________________

Instruction on the second coming 17:20-37

47. Where was the kingdom located that Christ was then establishing?

17:21 ______________________________

The phrase "within you" should be translated "in your midst" or "among you." The kingdom was in the midst of the Pharisees, not within them, in the person of the King, Christ Himself.

48. What form was the kingdom then being established in their midst to take until He should return to power?

19:11, 12; Acts 1:6-8; Romans 14:17 ______________________________

49. Why will it not be possible for fanatics to point here or there and say, "This is the second coming of Christ"?

17:24 ______________________________

50. When is "His day" (17:24)?

Acts 1:7 ______________________________

51. Why must Christ first suffer and be rejected (17:25)?

John 3:14, 15; I Peter 2:24 ______________________________

52. Compare Noah's day with the days preceding the second coming of Christ (17:26).

Genesis 6:12; 7:1; compare II Thessalonians 2:1-3 ______________________________

53. What should men learn from the story of God's indignation in the past (17:29)?

II Peter 3:7-9 ______________________________

54. In view of these facts, what should men do (17:30)?

I Peter 1:13 ______________________________

55. What will His coming mean for His saints?

II Thessalonians 1:7, 10 ______________________________

56. Why should we remember Lot's wife, that monument of God's wrath (17:32)?

I Corinthians 10:6 ______________________________

57. Why will Christ's coming be in the night to some people on the earth?

17:34 ______________________________

58. Why will it be full daytime for others, who are working in the fields?

17:36 ______________________________

The rotundity of the earth is clearly implied in these verses.

check-up time No. 8

You have just studied some important truths about service for Christ. Now take this test to see how well you understand important truths you have studied.

Circle the letter of the correct or most nearly correct answer.

1. The number of Christians that are stewards is (a) few, (b) many, (c) all.

2. The "mammon of unrighteousness" was (a) money, (b) men, (c) misery.

3. The treasurer of the disciples was (a) John, (b) Judas, (c) Peter.

4. Although heaven and earth may pass away, that which will remain is (a) God's Word, (b) man's word, (c) Satan's word.

5. Scripture teaches that a couple is to remain married until (a) a difficult problem arises, (b) an insurmountable problem arises, (c) the death of one of the mates.

6. The rich man in hades remembered (a) his brothers, (b) his testimony, (c) his deliverance.

7. One reason men will not accept salvation is because of (a) God's grace, (b) Satan's blinding, (c) the Spirit's convicting.

8. An offending brother should be approached in (a) rebuke, (b) meekness, (c) indifference.

9. The leper that thanked Christ was (a) a Jew, (b) a Samaritan, (c) a Pharisee.

10. The kingdom Christ was then establishing was located (a) in Jerusalem, (b) within the Pharisees, (c) among the Pharisees.

Turn to page 96 and check your answers.

Lesson 9

The Kingdom and the King

18:1—19:48

The triumphal entry of Christ (19:28-40) is the climax in the long-suffering of the Saviour with the nation Israel. Christ instructs concerning the coming kingdom and Himself as King in this section.

Teaching of the unjust judge 18:1-8

1. What should we do regularly and persistently?

18:1 ______

2. What should cause us to pray with persistence?

James 1:3-7 ______

3. No matter how long God delays, of what should we always be assured?

18:7; compare John 11:4; Romans 8:28 ______

The reference to faith in verse 8 is to the belief in the whole body of revealed truth (Jude 3).

Teaching on self-righteousness 18:9-14

4. Of what is a self-righteous man ignorant (18:9)?

Romans 10:3 ______

5. What is the only source of righteousness that is acceptable with God?

Philippians 3:9; I Corinthians 1:30 ______

6. What may a man have and still be lost (18:11)?

ROMANS 10:1, 2 ______

7. What may a man not have and still be eligible for salvation?

18:14 (compare GALATIANS 2:16) ______

8. How does God look upon the person who says, "I am holier than thou"?

ISAIAH 65:5 ______

9. Why could the publican not lift his eyes to heaven (18:13)?

PSALM 40:12 ______

10. What does the prayer "Be merciful" (literally "propitiated") really mean?

ROMANS 3:25 ______

11. What is the conclusion of this story?

ROMANS 3:28 ______

12. How must every man get his standing before God?

ROMANS 4:5 ______

Teaching on entering the kingdom 18:15-30

13. What must every adult become in order to be saved?

18:17; compare MATTHEW 18:3 ______

14. Just how simple does a man's faith need to become if he is to enter the kingdom?

PSALM 131:2 ______

15. By addressing Jesus as "Master" (literally "Teacher"), what is shown as to the young man's conception of Jesus (18:18)?

JOHN 3:2 ______

16. What was lacking in the young man's conception of Jesus?

18:19; compare John 1:14, 18; I Timothy 3:16 ________

17. Why did Jesus send this particular person to the law of Moses (18:20)?

Romans 3:19; 7:12, 13 ________

18. If a man has not perfectly kept the law, where does he stand (18:21)?

Galatians 3:10 ________

19. What is the only door of salvation left open to a man?

Galatians 3:13; Romans 8:3 ________

20. By mentioning this "one thing lacking" (18:22), what did Jesus show the man about his keeping of the law?

Exodus 20:17 ________

21. Why could not this man follow Jesus (18:23)?

16:13 ________

22. What is the deceitfulness of riches sure to do?

Matthew 13:22 ________

23. Who else was made sorrowful beside the young man?

18:24 ________

24. What is always the danger to a rich man?

I Timothy 6:9, 10 ________

25. What would have to occur if a camel should go through the eye of a needle (18:25)?

18:27 ________

The Greek word for rope is very much like the word for camel. Some believe a copyist's error had made it "camel." Others think the Needle's Eye gate of the city is referred to, where it was necessary for camels to squat down in order to pass through.

26. What does this imply as to the salvation of rich men?

Genesis 18:14; Jeremiah 32:17 ______

27. Instead of sacrificing in following Jesus, what had the disciples gained?

18:30 ______

28. What is of more value in this life than riches?

Psalm 37:16 ______

29. What is the crowning gift of all?

Romans 6:21-23 ______

Prediction of His death 18:31-34

30. What prophecy would all this ill treatment fulfill (18:33)?

Psalm 22:16 ______

Teaching of the blind man 18:35-43

31. Why could not the rebukes of men hinder the blind man (18:39)?

Jeremiah 29:13 ______

32. Why did Jesus want him to tell what he wanted (18:41)?

Philippians 4:6; Jeremiah 33:3 ______

33. What has similar faith accomplished for many since that day (18:42)?

Psalm 30:2 ______

Teaching to Zacchaeus 19:1-10

34. How did Jesus know the man's name (19:5)?

John 10:14 ______

35. With whom is Jesus always ready to come and abide?

John 14:23 ________________

36. What was the one constant strain of complaint against Jesus on the part of the scribes and Pharisees?

19:7; compare 5:30; 7:34, 39; 15:2; 18:9-14 ________________

37. What did it mean that salvation had come to his house (19:9)?

I Corinthians 6:11 ________________

38. How far did Jesus go to save the lost (19:10)?

Romans 5:6 ________________

Teaching of the postponed kingdom 19:11-27

39. What form did many of the Jews think the kingdom of God ought to take at that time?

19:11; compare John 6:15; Acts 1:6 ________________

40. What form did Jesus say it was to take?

John 18:36 ________________

41. Where is the far country where the nobleman has gone (19:12)?

Ephesians 1:19-21; I Peter 3:22 ________________

42. What is it to "occupy" until He comes (19:13)?

I Thessalonians 1:9, 10 ________________

43. Upon what basis will His servants be judged (19:15)?

I Corinthians 3:13, 14 ________________

44. Of what will every Christian who has been faithful in His service, be assured (19:17)?

II Timothy 4:7, 8 ________________

45. How does the number of cities given each servant compare with the number of pounds gained?

19:18, 19 ______________________________

46. What reason have we to believe that we shall be given as much dominion as our faithfulness in service makes us capable of exercising?

I CORINTHIANS 3:8; 15:58 ______________________________

47. What was the real trouble with this last servant (19:20)?

PROVERBS 26:15, 16 ______________________________

48. What is the only way a person can have anything (19:24)?

MATTHEW 6:20, 21 ______________________________

49. If one does not grasp opportunities for God, what will happen?

19:26; compare PSALM 109:8 ______________________________

The triumphal entry 19:28-40

50. Why did Jesus want the ass's colt (19:30)?

JOHN 12:14, 15 ______________________________

51. Why did our Lord allow Himself to be in need of anything (19:34)?

II CORINTHIANS 8:9 ______________________________

52. How does the explanation concerning peace (19:38) compare with that mentioned by the angels at Jesus' birth?

2:14 ______________________________

LUKE 2:14 should be rendered, "Peace on earth to men of good will."

53. How was the peace to be made?

COLOSSIANS 1:20 ______________________________

The tears over Jerusalem 19:41-44

54. What were the things that belonged to their peace, which the Jews failed to see (19:42)?

1:78, 79; Acts 10:36; Romans 5:1 ______________________

55. In what did the national rejection of Christ by Israel result?

Romans 11:25 ______________________

56. To what does verse 43 refer?

21:20 ______________________

57. How low would Jerusalem be laid?

19:44; compare Micah 3:12 ______________________

The purification of the temple 19:45-48

58. Will Israel have a house that will not be a den of thieves (19:46)?

Isaiah 56:7 ______________________

59. To what did the chief priests and scribes resort, in the effort to find something against Jesus (19:47)?

20:20 ______________________

60. What did they finally have to do?

Matthew 26:59 ______________________

check-up time No. 9

You have just studied some important truths about the kingdom and the King. Review your study by rereading the questions and your written answers. If you wish, you may use the self-check test as an aid in reviewing your lesson. If you aren't sure of an answer, reread the Scripture portion given to see if you can find the answer. Then take this test to see how well you understand important truths you have studied.

In the right-hand margin write "True" or "False" after each of the following statements.

1. One reason Christians should pray is because Christ commanded us to do so. T
2. The Pharisee wanted God to be merciful to him because he was a sinner. F
3. God may sometimes accept our own righteousness as merit for our salvation. F
4. Jesus showed the ruler who asked Him how to inherit eternal life that He was only a good man. F
5. It is easy for a rich man to fall into temptation. T
6. In following Jesus, the disciples sacrificed more than they gained. F
7. Christ predicted His being mocked, scourged, and spit upon, as well as His death and resurrection. T
8. The reason Christ came was to seek and to save the lost. T
9. Jesus wanted to ride on the colt because He was very tired. F
10. The leaders of Israel tried hard to find a flaw in Christ. T

Turn to page 96 and check your answers.

LESSON 10

The Opposition to Christ

20:1—21:38

Although the religious leaders had opposed Christ previously, their increased opposition is seen in this section preparatory to the crucifixion.

The opposition of the priests 20:1-26

1. What was the gospel that Jesus preached (20:1)?

MATTHEW 20:28; LUKE 24:27 ______________________________

2. Where did Jesus get His authority (20:2)?

JOHN 5:22-25 ______________________________

3. Of whom had John the Baptist, whom the people knew to be a prophet, testified (20:6)?

JOHN 1:15-18, 30, 34 ______________________________

4. When such men resist the truth of God, what is proved about them (20:7)?

II TIMOTHY 3:8 ______________________________

5. What did Jesus' answer (20:8) prove them to be?

PROVERBS 26:5 ______________________________

6. What nation, divinely planted, is likened to a vineyard (20:9)?

ISAIAH 5:1-7 ______________________________

7. Who are the husbandmen?

Deuteronomy 1:15-18 ____________________

8. For what does the servant first sent by Jehovah stand (20:10)?

II Kings 17:13 ____________________

9. What did the Jews do to the prophets who were sent them?

Matthew 23:30-37 ____________________

10. To whom does the beloved son refer (20:13)?

Hebrews 1:1, 2 ____________________

11. What had been prophesied concerning the attitude of these rulers toward the Lord's Anointed (20:14)?

Psalm 2:2 ____________________

12. Who, within a very short time, said, "Let us kill him"?

20:19; compare 19:47 ____________________

13. To what does the casting out of the vineyard refer (20:15)?

Acts 2:23 ____________________

14. What had Daniel foreseen would follow the cutting off of the Messiah (20:16)?

Daniel 9:26 ____________________

15. To whom has the vineyard now been let out?

Romans 11:11 ____________________

16. How did the apostles apply the Scripture concerning the stone set at nought of the builders (20:17)?

Acts 4:10, 11 ____________________

17. Why had these leaders failed a number of times to get their hands upon Him (20:19)?

John 7:30 ____________________

18. What was ridiculous about their efforts to deliver the Son of God into the power of men (20:20)?

Psalm 66:3 ______

19. If they knew that Jesus taught rightly, of what were they proved guilty (20:21)?

II Corinthians 2:17 ______

20. What had happened to one man who had taught the people that they ought not to contribute to Caesar's government (20:22)?

Acts 5:37 ______

21. Where does a Christian have a citizenship, besides heaven, with duties toward it?

20:25; compare Romans 13:1-7 ______

22. What did they finally learn about their ability to entangle Jesus?

20:26; compare 20:40 ______

The opposition of the Sadducees 20:27-38

23. Why cannot those in heaven die any more (20:36)?

I Corinthians 15:26, 57 ______

24. What will it mean to have the privileges of angels?

Zechariah 3:7; Revelation 5:9-14 ______

25. Why did Jesus bring in this argument about the resurrection?

20:27 ______

The opposition of the scribes 20:39-47

26. In what sense only was Jesus the Son of David (20:44)?
Acts 13:22, 23; Romans 1:3; 9:5 ______

27. What one thing will aggravate the suffering of the lost above everything else?

20:46, 47; compare JOB 8:13 ____________________

The offering of the widow 21:1-4

28. In accordance with what is our giving to be done (21:1)?

I CORINTHIANS 16:2 ____________________

29. Why had the widow cast in more than the rich men (21:3)?

II CORINTHIANS 8:12 ____________________

30. What had she done more than the others?

21:4; compare 18:12 ____________________

The overthrow of Jerusalem 21:5-38

31. What had Jeremiah foreseen (21:6)?

JEREMIAH 7:11-14 ____________________

32. Why was this pronounced upon them?

19:44 ____________________

33. By what means will men be deceived as to the course and end of the age?

21:8; compare II CORINTHIANS 11:13-15 ____________________

34. Why will wars continue throughout this age?

21:9; compare JAMES 4:1 ____________________

35. What will be the Christian's attitude in all these turmoils?

PSALM 27:3, 4 ____________________

36. How will all the commotions among nations culminate (21: 10)?

ZECHARIAH 14:2, 3; REVELATION 6:4-12 ____________________

37. When will the signs in the heavens take place (21:11)?

Matthew 24:29 ______________________________

38. What attitude toward Christ's witnesses will be characteristic of the last days?

21:12; compare II Peter 3:3 ______________________________

39. In what will patience and faith in such times surely result?

21:13; compare II Thessalonians 1:4, 5 ______________________________

40. For what kind of occasions are Christian workers not to prepare?

21:14, 15; compare Matthew 10:19 ______________________________

41. Who evidently claimed this promise of Jesus?

Acts 6:8-10 ______________________________

42. What is very apt to be true in the lives of Christian workers?

21:16; compare Micah 7:6 ______________________________

43. What do Christian workers need to learn, as well as the doing of God's will?

21:19; compare Hebrews 10:36 ______________________________

44. What was to follow immediately the siege of Jerusalem carried out under Titus in A.D. 70?

21:20, 24 ______________________________

45. What is to follow immediately the coming siege as predicted in Matthew's account?

Matthew 24: 29, 30 ______________________________

46. What is going to happen for Israel when Christ comes back to reign?

Jeremiah 31:31-34 ______________________________

47. Compare Isaiah's forecast of the coming day of the Lord with verse 25.

ISAIAH 13:9, 10 ______________________________

48. What should the thought that Christ is coming soon to set the world right give rise to in the Christian's heart (21:28)?

PSALM 98:7-9 ______________________________

49. What redemption is yet future?

ROMANS 8:19-23; EPHESIANS 1:14; 4:30 ______________

50. When we see the evident signs of the fulfillment of prophecy, what should it cause us to do (21:31)?

JAMES 5:7-9 ______________________________

51. Why has not the generation (literally "race" or "stock") of Israel become extinct through these centuries?

21:32; compare ISAIAH 54:7, 8 ______________________

52. What effect should the hope of the Lord's coming have upon believers?

21:34; compare II PETER 3:11; I THESSALONIANS 5:5, 6 ________

53. Who are those who shall escape the coming tribulation period and stand before the Son of man (21:36)?

I THESSALONIANS 4:16, 17 ______________________

check-up time No. 10

You have just studied some important truths about the opposition to Christ. Now take this test to see how well you understand important truths you have studied.

Circle the letter of the correct or most nearly correct answer.

1. John the Baptist had testified of (a) himself, (b) Christ, (c) Moses.

2. The nation that is likened to a vineyard is (a) Israel, (b) Babylon, (c) Rome.

3. Daniel predicted that following the cutting off of Messiah would come (a) the Babylonian empire, (b) the second coming of Christ, (c) the destruction of Jerusalem.

4. The vineyard has now been let out to (a) Gentiles, (b) Satan, (c) Israel.

5. After the chief priests and scribes were answered by Christ, they (a) became his followers, (b) stoned Him, (c) marveled at Him.

6. Jesus taught the resurrection to the Sadducees because they (a) depended on it, (b) denied it, (c) disagreed about it.

7. Our giving is to be in accordance with our (a) position, (b) purpose, (c) prospering.

8. In the last days, Christ's witnesses will be (a) Christians, (b) persecuted, (c) Jews only.

9. Immediately following the siege of Jerusalem (A.D. 70), there was to be (a) desolation, (b) darkness, (c) drought.

10. The believer's hope of the Lord's return is intended to (a) teach him curious things, (b) purify his life, (c) make him proud.

Turn to page 96 and check your answers.

LESSON 11

The Betrayal to the Burial of Christ

22:1—23:56

The rejection of Christ is climaxed in His crucifixion. In this section, Luke describes this as well as the intense passion of the Son of Man.

The solicitation to betray Christ 22:1-6

1. As the Jews prepared their Passover sacrifice, what did they fail to see was about to take place (22:1)?

I CORINTHIANS 5:7 ____________________

2. What were they unconsciously doing (22:2)?

ISAIAH 53:7 ____________________

3. What was the real nature that had been dominating Judas for some time?

22:3; compare JOHN 6:70 ____________________

4. How was verse 5 to fulfill the Scripture?

ZECHARIAH 11:12 ____________________

5. Why did Judas want to betray Jesus in the absence of the multitude (22:6)?

MATTHEW 26:5 ____________________

The supper of Christ 22:7-46

The Jewish day began at sundown, so that the slaying of the Passover lamb was the beginning of the day of unleavened bread.

6. At what time of day would the Passover lamb be killed on the fourteenth day of the month (22:7)?

EXODUS 12:6 ______________________________

7. On what day did Jesus hang upon the cross?

JOHN 19:31, 42 ______________________________

The real Passover feast, on the fifteenth of Nisan, had to be eaten standing. There were several preparatory meals, not really a part of the feast, but through custom classified as part of the Passover celebration itself. This is why Jesus could eat the Passover and yet hang on the cross the evening before the feast (EXODUS 12:11; MATTHEW 26:20).

8. What had the owner of the guest chamber evidently been led of God to do (22:12)?

MARK 14:15 ______________________________

9. Why was it necessary that Christ eat the Passover with His disciples before His suffering (22:15)?

Leviticus 23:5, 6 ______________________________

10. Of what does this cup speak (22:17)?

PSALM 116:13 ______________________________

11. When will the kingdom of God fully come (22:18)?

REVELATION 22:12, 20 ______________________________

12. What is the believer to be careful to discern when partaking of the Lord's supper (22:19)?

I CORINTHIANS 11:29 ______________________________

13. In what sense only can we partake of Christ?

GALATIANS 2:20 ______________________________

14. How long will this covenant sealed with the blood of Christ stand (22:20)?

HEBREWS 13:20 ______________________________

15. What significance was the fact that Judas' hand was with that of Christ on the table (22:21)?

PSALM 41:9 ______________________________

16. What is the only course to take in order to get to be "chief" (22:26)?

9:48 ______________________________

17. In what sense are believers to have a kingdom (22:29)?

II TIMOTHY 2:12; JAMES 2:5 ______________________________

18. What special privilege is to be given the chosen twelve?

22:30 ______________________________

19. Who will have part in the judgment of the world?

I CORINTHIANS 6:2 ______________________________

20. Give the reason for believing that no true child of God can be lost through Satan's testings (22:32).

HEBREWS 7:25; ROMANS 8:34 ______________________________

21. Compare Peter's boast (22:33) with what he wrote afterward.

I PETER 5:10 ______________________________

22. With what kind of sword is the Christian called to fight (22:36)?

EPHESIANS 6:17 ______________________________

23. If we receive Jesus who was reckoned among the transgressors, what is reckoned to us (22:37)?

ROMANS 4:24, 25 ______________________________

24. What prayer did some of the disciples need to be praying at this time?

22:40; compare PSALM 17:5 ______________________________

25. What symptom of approaching death was seen in the garden?

22:44 ______________________________

26. How was Christ's prayer for the Father's will answered (22:42)?

22:43; compare HEBREWS 5:7 ____________________

27. How many times did Jesus go away and pray in Gethsemane (22:45)?

MARK 14:41 ____________________

The sentencing of Christ 22:47—23:25

28. What was the abominable part of Judas' act (22:48)?

ACTS 1:17 ____________________

29. Who cut off the servant's ear (22:50)?

JOHN 18:10 ____________________

30. What was Jesus' last miracle before His crucifixion?

22:51 ____________________

31. Why was there no need of their men coming after Him with swords and staves (22:52)?

22:37 ____________________

32. What might have kept Peter from danger (22:54)?

PSALM 37:31 ____________________

33. In what class did Peter put himself by sitting among the men in the hall (22:55)?

PSALM 1:1 ____________________

34. Compare Peter's action (22:57) with his previous boasting.

22:33 ____________________

35. Why should the crowing of the cock have convicted Peter?

22:33, 34, 60 ____________________

36. What may the look of an eye accomplish (22:61)?

PSALM 32:8 ____________________

37. What upholds every true child of God who fails in hours of weakness?

HEBREWS 7:25; JOHN 17:20 ______

38. What was Jesus' appearance after the mob was through with Him (22:65)?

ISAIAH 52:14 ______

39. Why did Jesus have no desire to argue with them?

22:67; compare 22:37 ______

40. Where is Christ now?

22:69; compare Hebrews 1:3; 12:2 ______

41. Why could not Pilate find any fault in him (23:4)?

HEBREWS 7:26 ______

42. Since when had Herod been desirous of seeing Jesus (23:8)?

9:9 ______

43. What will mutual antipathy toward Christ often accomplish?

PSALM 83:5 ______

44. Why did Pilate have to release a prisoner (23:17)?

MATTHEW 27:15 ______

45. What crime had Barabbas committed?

23:19; compare ACTS 3:14 ______

46. What caused Pilate to sentence Jesus?

23:24, 25; compare JOHN 19:12, 13 ______

The sacrifice of Christ 23:26-56

47. When will men desire the mountains to fall upon them (23:30)?

REVELATION 6:14-17; 9:6 ______

48. How had the manner of Jesus' death been predicted (23:33)?

PSALM 22:16 ______________________________

49. What was being accomplished for the world?

I PETER 2:24; GALATIANS 3:13 ______________________________

50. Why could Christ not save Himself (23:35)?

JOHN 3:14 ______________________________

51. What truth did Pilate unwittingly tell by putting the title on the cross (23:38)?

1:32 ______________________________

52. What had this malefactor evidently come to see in regard to Christ?

23:41; I PETER 2:22 ______________________________

53. What had the man gained for himself by this simple confession (23:42)?

12:8 ______________________________

54. From which direction was the veil of the temple rent (23:45)?

MATTHEW 27:51 ______________________________

55. What did this indicate?

HEBREWS 9:3-8, 11-17; 10:19-22 ______________________________

56. What was indicated by the power Jesus had to dismiss His own spirit (23:46)?

JOHN 10:18 ______________________________

57. When did the women bring their fragrant spices (23:56)?

24:1 ______________________________

58. Why was Jesus' body never embalmed?

ACTS 2:24-31 ______________________________

check-up time No. 11

You have just studied some important truths about the events of the crucifixion of Christ. Review your study by rereading the questions and your written answers. If you wish, you may use the self-check test as an aid in reviewing your lesson. If you aren't sure of an answer, reread the Scripture portion given to see if you can find the answer. Then take this test to see how well you understand important truths you have studied.

In the right-hand margin write "True" or "False" after each of the following statements.

1. The betrayal of Christ for thirty pieces of silver was predicted in the Old Testament. T
2. Believers will reign with Christ in the coming kingdom. T
3. In the garden, the disciples were to pray for the deliverance of Christ. F
4. Angels from heaven ministered to Christ in the garden. T
5. Judas was never considered a disciple of Christ. F
6. Judas cut off the ear of the servant of the high priest. F
7. Although Jesus argued His case before the Sanhedrin, they sent Him to Pilate. F
8. Herod was reluctant to see Christ. F
9. The veil of the temple was rent from top to bottom. T
10. The body of Jesus did not see corruption. T

Turn to page 96 and check your answers.

The Resurrection and Ascension of Christ

24:1-53

A biography generally ends with the death of that person, but this is not so with the biography of Christ. This is the chapter after the death of Christ with His promises to the disciples and us today.

The resurrection of Christ 24:1-12

1. On what day of the week was light called forth?

GENESIS 1:3, 5 ______________________________

2. What greater Light was called forth on the first day of the week?

24:1-3; compare II TIMOTHY 1:10 ______________________________

3. From this time forward, what day of the week was observed by the apostles and early church?

ACTS 20:7 ______________________________

4. What did Paul say about the old Sabbath?

COLOSSIANS 2:14-17 ______________________________

5. Who was now the first witness of completed redemption?

23:55; 24:1 ______________________________

6. What word of Jesus was now fulfilled (24:3)?

JOHN 10:18 ______________________________

7. Whom did the women find in the sepulchre?

MARK 16:5 ______________________________

8. Of what is Jesus' resurrection the pledge?

I CORINTHIANS 15:20-22 ______

9. What illustration that Jesus had used of His coming resurrection was recalled to the disciples' minds (24:8)?

JOHN 2:18-22 ______

10. Which one of these women first saw Jesus after His resurrection (24:10)?

MARK 16:9 ______

11. What happened as the women were on their way to tell the disciples?

MATTHEW 28:9, 10 ______

12. What rebuke did the disciples get for their slowness in believing the story (24:11)?

24:25 ______

13. Who ran to the sepulchre with Peter (24:12)?

JOHN 20:3, 4 ______

The revelation of Christ 24:13-32

14. Why were these two followers of Jesus sad (24:17)?

JOHN 16:4-6 ______

15. What had Jesus prophesied about their sorrow?

JOHN 16:20, 21 ______

16. Who was Cleopas' wife (24:18)?

JOHN 19:25 ______

17. Of what redemption only were these men thinking?

24:21; compare ACTS 1:6 ______

18. What wider redemption had Jesus come to provide?

John 1:29 ______________________________

19. What did these disciples think the women had seen?

24:23 ______________________________

20. Why was it necessary for Jesus to have suffered these things (24:26)?

Hebrews 2:9-11 ______________________________

21. What had been prophesied about His resurrection (24:27)?

Psalm 16:9, 10 ______________________________

22. What is the whole spirit of the prophecies?

Revelation 19:10 ______________________________

23. What has Jesus promised to do for each one of His followers (24:29)?

John 14:23 ______________________________

24. What may we all have our eyes opened to behold (24:31)?

Psalm 119:18 ______________________________

25. What else may be revealed to us?

Galatians 1:16 ______________________________

26. When will our eyes look upon Christ as He is?

I John 3:2 ______________________________

27. What feeling may we have in our hearts for Christ although we have not seen Him?

24:32; compare I Peter 1:8 ______________________________

28. What is a greater blessedness than to have seen Him with our physical eyes?

John 20:29-31 ______________________________

The announcements of Christ 24:33-49

29. What two disciples are known to have been absent from this meeting (24:33)?

ACTS 1:25; JOHN 20:24 ________________________________

Dr. Scofield says that the designation "the eleven" was a collective term equivalent to saying, "the band of disciples," or the "Sanhedrin," or "the commons," not necessarily implying the eleven were present at the meeting. I Corinthians 15:5 refers to "the twelve" although Paul knew there were not twelve actually present. Note MATTHEW 28:16, where it is distinctly said that there were "eleven disciples" present.

30. What did Christ show the disciples about their own condition of heart (24:36)?

MARK 16:14 ________________________________

31. At what other time had they taken Him for a spirit (24:37)?

MARK 6:49 ________________________________

32. How did He know what was in their hearts (24:38)?

HEBREWS 4:13 ________________________________

33. Why did He not say "flesh and blood" (24:39)?

I CORINTHIANS 15:50 ________________________________

Blood is to repair the waste in our mortal bodies—hence the combination of flesh and blood will no longer exist. Jesus had flesh and bones. The divine Spirit evidently takes the place of blood.

34. What is in contrast to their believing not for joy (24:41)?

22:45 ________________________________

35. How is it definitely proved that the resurrection of Jesus was no mere vision and that He was no mere spirit?

24:43; compare ACTS 10:40, 41 ________________________________

36. What three divisions were there in the Old Testament?

24:44 ______

37. Who must open our hearts if we would understand the Scriptures?

24:45; compare ACTS 16:14 ______

38. How were the disciples able to strengthen their testimony concerning Jesus?

24:48; compare ACTS 1:21, 22; 2:32 ______

39. Where did they begin witnessing?

ACTS 1:8 ______

40. What were they to teach all nations? Baptizing them in the Name of the Father son + The Holy Ghost

MATTHEW 28:19, 20 Make Disciples of all Nations

41. What was the promise of the Father (24:49)?

JOHN 14:16, 17; 15:26; 16:7-16 He will never leave you nor forsake

42. When did the power come?

ACTS 2:1-4 After the Holy Spirit fell upon them

43. What command is given us all?

EPHESIANS 5:18 Give thanks to God the Father for everything In The Name of Jesus Christ

The ascension of Christ 24:50-53

44. What was Jesus' first action when He met His disciples in resurrection?

24:36 ______

45. What was His last action before He returned to glory?

24:50 ______

46. What will be His next action when He comes?

I PETER 5:4 ____________________

47. In what manner did Jesus disappear?

24:51; compare ACTS 1:9, 10 ____________________

48. What definite promise was made from heaven when He left?

ACTS 1:11 ____________________

49. What could the disciples then have said?

PSALM 30:11 ____________________

50. If they could only have believed what Jesus said in the first place, what would they have done all the time?

JOHN 14:28 ____________________

51. What was the effect of the resurrection upon the early church?

24:53; compare ACTS 2:46 They worship

52. What did it cause them to do persistently?

ACTS 5:42 Preach Jesus is the Messiah

53. If we follow their example, what promise of Jesus have we?

MATTHEW 28:20 He is with us always
even to the end of the age.

check-up time No. 12

You have just studied some important truths about the resurrection and ascension of Christ. Now take this test to see how well you understand important truths you have studied.

Circle the letter of the correct or most nearly correct answer.

1. Christ was raised from the dead on (a) the Sabbath, (b) Sunday, (c) the Passover.

2. The first witnesses to the empty tomb were (a) women, (b) disciples, (c) Pharisees.

3. The resurrection of Christ is the pledge of (a) eternal hell, (b) the Holy Spirit, (c) our resurrection.

4. The first disciple to the empty tomb was (a) Peter, (b) Paul, (c) John.

5. The companions to Emmaus thought the women had seen (a) a vision, (b) a phantom, (c) the Saviour.

6. The two disciples absent when Christ first appeared to them after His resurrection were (a) James and John, (b) Judas and Thomas, (c) Thomas and Peter.

7. One proof that Christ's resurrection was not a vision was His (a) eating and drinking, (b) appearing to the women, (c) appearing to the disciples.

8. The disciples began their witnessing in (a) Judea, (b) Samaria, (c) Jerusalem.

9. The last action of Christ before He returned to glory was His (a) drinking with the disciples, (b) blessing of the disciples, (c) speaking to the disciples.

10. The angels at Christ's ascension promised His (a) return, (b) Spirit, (c) blessing.

Turn to page 96 and check your answers.

Suggestions for class use

---

1. The class teacher may wish to tear this page from each workbook as the answer key is on the reverse side.

2. The teacher should study the lesson first, filling in the blanks in the workbook. He should be prepared to give help to the class on some of the harder places in the lesson. He should also take the self-check tests himself, check his answers with the answer key and look up any question answered incorrectly.

3. Class sessions can be supplemented by the teacher's giving a talk or leading a discussion on the subject to be studied. The class could then fill in the workbook together as a group, in teams, or individually. If so desired by the teacher, however, this could be done at home. The self-check tests can be done as homework by the class.

4. The self-check tests can be corrected at the beginning of each class session. A brief discussion of the answers can serve as review for the previous lesson.

5. The teacher should motivate and encourage his students. Some public recognition might well be given to class members who successfully complete this course.

Moody Press, a ministry of the Moody Bible Institute, is designed for education, evangelization and edification. If we may assist you in knowing more about Christ and the Christian life, please write us without obligation to:
Moody Press, c/o MLM, Chicago, Illinois 60610.

answer key
to self-check tests

Be sure to look up any questions you answered incorrectly.

A gives the correct *answer.*

R refers you back to the number of the question in the lesson itself, where the correct answer is to be found.

Mark with an "x" your wrong answers.

	TEST 1		TEST 2		TEST 3		TEST 4		TEST 5		TEST 6	
Question	*A*	*R*	*A*	*R*	*A*	*R*	*A*	*R*	*A*	*R*	*A*	*R*
1	F	6	b	2	T	1	b	2	F	5	c	1
2	F	6	a	7	T	5	c	12	T	7	b	8
3	T	9	c	9	T	8	c	15	F	11	a	17
4	T	17	a	14	F	14	a	32	T	16	b	19
5	T	19	b	19	F	18	b	34	T	26	c	22
6	T	24	c	25	T	21	c	36	F	28	a	24
7	F	39	a	33	F	35	b	48	F	33	b	36
8	T	40	b	36	T	42	a	53	T	36	c	38
9	F	46	a	38	F	49	b	61	T	48	c	44
10	F	49	c	48	F	56	a	68	F	57	a	51

	TEST 7		TEST 8		TEST 9		TEST 10		TEST 11		TEST 12	
Question	*A*	*R*	*A*	*R*	*A*	*R*	*A*	*R*	*A*	*R*	*A*	*R*
1	T	7	c	1	T	1	b	3	T	4	b	2
2	T	14	a	9	F	9	a	6	T	17	a	5
3	F	15	b	12	F	12	c	14	F	24	c	8
4	T	24	a	19	F	16	a	15	T	26	c	13
5	F	27	c	21	T	24	c	22	F	28	a	19
6	T	30	a	30	F	27	b	25	F	29	b	29
7	T	35	b	32	T	30	c	28	F	39	a	35
8	F	37	b	36	T	38	b	38	F	42	c	39
9	F	44	b	43	F	50	a	44	T	54	b	45
10	T	49	c	47	T	59	b	52	T	58	a	48

How well did you do?

0-1 wrong answers—excellent work

2-3 wrong answers—review errors carefully

4 or more wrong answers—restudy the lesson before going on to the next one